The Easter Victory

The Story of Easter
Matthew 26–28 for children

Written by Erik Rottmann

Illustrated by Paige Billin-Frye

CONCORDIA PUBLISHING HOUSE • SAINT LOUIS

One mournful Friday afternoon
Outside the city wall,
The Son of God was crucified
For sinners one and all.

By Jewish law, each Friday was
The day all work must cease
Before the Saturday of rest
To hear God's Word of peace.

On this sad Friday, Jesus died.
He finished everything
The Father sent Him here to do.
Hosanna to our King!

Jesus Christ, the Son of God
Began His work for you
When, by the Spirit of the Lord,
He entered Mary's womb.

His work continued with His birth
Inside a cattle stall.
Mary laid Him in the hay,
So soft and pink and small.

When fully grown, Christ labored on
In healing for the blind;
In preaching Good News to the poor;
In actions pure and kind.

One Thursday, after Jesus gave
Communion to His friends,
They ran away and left their Lord
Abandoned in the end.

They ran because some angry men
Tied Jesus' hands and feet.
They kicked and hit and spat on Him
Then dragged Him down the street.

On Friday morning, Jesus stood
At Pilate's judgment place.
Then Jesus suffered whips and blows
And slaps upon His face.

But all of this He gladly bore,
And willingly He died.
He earned salvation full and free
When He was crucified.

"It is finished," Jesus cried
That Friday afternoon.
A man named Joseph took Him down
And laid Him in a tomb.

By Jewish law, each Friday was
The day all work must cease.
So Jesus had a Sabbath rest,
His labor now complete.

The week is done! Salvation's won!
In Sunday morning light
The Son of God rose from the dead.
Oh, what a joyous sight!

Your Lord's great work of suffering
Was taken up for you.
You now possess the gift of life
Because His work is through.

You now have Jesus' holiness.
Sin's debt has been released.
Because of Jesus' death and life
You have God's Word of peace.

Through every Sunday morning's Word,
Through water, wine and bread
God's people are assured that they
Shall rise up from the dead.

Dear Parents,

From the moment of His conception to His last breath on the cross, every step of Jesus' life was a measured, deliberate step taken for the purpose of earning your salvation. The resurrection joy of Easter dawn anticipates your own participation—and your child's participation—in the future joy of eternal, resurrected life with Him. "Do you not know that all of us who have been baptized into Christ Jesus were baptized into His death? We were buried therefore with Him by baptism into death, in order that, just as Christ was raised from the dead by the glory of the Father, we too might walk in the newness of life. For if we have been united with Him in a death like His, we shall certainly be united with Him in a resurrection like His" (Romans 6:3–5).

Use this story of Holy Week to proclaim to your child that Christ completed everything needed for your child's salvation. Perhaps you could even teach your child the ancient Christian greeting, "Christ is risen!" with its response, "He is risen indeed!" Then give thanks to God together that, because Jesus fully completed the work He was sent to do, you both now have the benefits of eternal life in Him.

The Author